A Dog's Tail

Kashvi Silswal

Copyright © 2017 Kashvi Silswal

All Rights Reserved.

This book is a work of fiction. Names, characters, places, and incidents are either products of the author's imagination or are used fictitiously. Any resemblance to actual events or locales or persons (human or canine), living or dead, is entirely coincidental.

Proofreading & Editing
by
Cupboardy Wordsmithing

Table of Contents

Acknowledgements vii
Introduction 1
My First Day Home 3
The Bells 7
My Appetite 11
The Gold Mine 13
The Broken Keyboard 15
The Great Glorious Escapes 19
People 23
Wild Side 25
Who's the Bully? 29
Are You Leaving? 33
Owner Sick 35
A High Percent of Showers 39
A Wild Feast 41
I'm Tired 43
Mattress Mining 45
You Wanna Fight, Short-Pants? 47
Ms. Annoying-Pants 49

Doses of Poison	51
Who is That??!!	53
Mine!	55
Scat Exploration	57
Secret Spy Hideouts	59
Bugged by Ticks	61
Rules of Engagement	63
Matchi Mansion	65
I Could Use Some Help	69
The Food Frightening Dreams	73
The Bunnies Did It!	77
A Sweet Treat	81
I See You	85
Aim 'n' ... Fire!	87
Gas Engine	90
The Fun Prison	92
Cat in My Throat	96
Guardian of the Peaches	98
Acid Rain	101
Weed Feed	105

Limbo!	109
The Change in Diet	113
Taxi!	117
What a Shocker	121
Bunnies Are Buddies	125
Drag Racing	129
Take Me Out for a Run	133
Yawn	137
A Slice of Paradise	139
A Close Encounter	143
Own the Throne	147
My Schooling	151
Top Dog	155
There's a Pit Bull on the Loose	159
Birthday Bash	161
Small Spaces	163
Surprise Attack	167
Missed Opportunity	171
Bye-Bye	175
Afterword: Author's Note	177

Acknowledgements

Not to get all mushy-gushy and all but there are a few people I would like to give a shout out to. Like my dad & mom who supported me all the way, and my dog, who inspired this book with his crazy spirit and friendly demeanor. Without him I couldn't live and write this book. My parents, also, for funding the whole project while paying the bills and feeding the dog. And I can't forget my lightning quick editor, David. Not only did he edit the book but, he also mentored me in a way. I guess that's it. Wait! I almost forgot, *you*, for reading this book you're holding in your hands and for believing in this crazy dog.

Introduction

Have you ever wondered what is going on in your dog's head? I'm...

Matchi

... a dog that loves food ⊃ a lot! I am a beagle. I am part of a group of dogs called "hounds." You might think a dog's life is so easy with the eating, sleeping, playing, and eating some more. Let me give you the grand tour of my life as a dog. But before we dive in, let me tell you some important facts about dogs — we love food, and we can't stand cats, birds, fences, etc.

Also, hounds bark at people. It's what we do.

A DOG'S TAIL

P.S. "Hound" is a mix between *happy* and *loud* but people added the "n" for "nice." It's true!

My First Day Home

I remember when I first got to what I now call home. Once I got there, all I wanted to do was sleep.

After about an hour, I was lifted up into the air by my owner. Then we went outside and greeted some people (to tell you the truth, I was pretty freaked out at first, but then got used to it). Oh, and when I

A DOG'S TAIL

say people, I mean *people* people, not dog people.

Just so you know, my human mom, dad, brother, and sister adopted me — or, hey, maybe I adopted them! Either way, I'm stuck with them and they're stuck with me — but it's all right. They're my pack now.

Okay, so then I went inside and explored the house a bit. Then, it was time for dinner (my favorite part of the day). After that, I looked around to find some toys. I found a tug-of-war toy and made my owners play with me.

This little girl came in the room next and I was like, "Who are you?"

She started petting me and cooed *"Who's a good boy?"* over and over again and I was like, "I'm a good boy," over and over again.

Why she kept asking me when I answered her the first time, I don't know. But she was pretty nice and I liked her, so I didn't mind so much.

After a little bit of play, I went to sleep.

A DOG'S TAIL

The Bells

A few weeks after my first day at home, I found some bells near the door. Mostly, I use the bells to go out and talk loudly to stranger-dangers and also to occasionally do my real business.

When I first got them, though, my dad tried to teach me when and how to use the bells but I didn't listen. It's not my fault! Don't blame me as I was focused on food. See,

A DOG'S TAIL

my mom was cooking a nice stew and at times she uses me as a taste-tester!

So while my dad was trying to teach me, I got the idea of these bells mixed up in my head with food —because I was distracted by food, like anyone would be — and I thought, "Hey, could I use these bells to get some food I want? Is that what Dad's trying to tell me? Because, if so, that would be pretty awesome!"

If that worked, it would be like they were my butlers!

So I tried the bells out by pawing at them and, yeah, once I tried it out I realized they could understand me that way and then they'd let me outside to pee and stuff.

But not to give me food.

It didn't work like that.

Which is okay, I guess.

Though of course I liked my original idea about the food better. And them being my butlers.

My Appetite

So today I woke up to a smell — the smelliest of all smells. Smelly in a good way, I mean. So I decided to follow the scent of this particular smell. (Did I use "particular" right? I'm still learning all the human words).

What I found was glorious! It was beautiful! One word:

A DOG'S TAIL

There was food cooking and people eating food. Then it was my turn to eat. I couldn't wait!

Then I got my food! **Yesss!**

But mine was kibble. Again. **WWWHHHYYY?!?!?**

I'd been having kibble for what felt like a *century* already.

(C'mon. Seriously?!?!?)

The Gold Mine

One day while my pack was out for a day-long soccer game, I had lot of time to explore.

I found a mine!

Don't get me wrong, this wasn't a gold mine — not like that — but pretty close!

I found out the people I live with are hoarders! They have all sorts of old stuff: books, tables,

A DOG'S TAIL

chairs, pictures, etc. But most importantly... toys! Lots of them! Some of them even squeak!

I found a porcupine — a squeaky one (I told you) — and I played with him all day and guess what? By the next day, he was gone!

Weird. I loved that porcupine.

shrugs

Well, 1 down, about 100 more to go!

The Broken Keyboard

One person in the family was having a sleepover so I was like, "Count me in!" We played video games, ate pizza (although I didn't get much), and played on laptops.

The next morning, we played some more video games. Then it was time for breakfast (I got my usual — kibble). I gobbled that down and decided to enjoy the smell of glory (food!).

I got bored, so, in search of more food I went to the living room where the laptops were. I smelled more food and it was coming from one laptop. I dug and dug. I found food crumbs under the keys!

Yes!

Once my owners found out about this, they were furious and sent me to my kennel.

You'd think they'd be happy that I cleaned up the laptops, right?

But no.

A DOG'S TAIL

The Great Glorious Escapes

I've been trapped in this prison, my people call it home, for what feels like centuries! I believe it's time to make my escape! I'm ready and I know I can do it! I was out going pee when I thought up an idea.

I tried it out and it worked!

I was free to do whatever I wanted. So I decided to find food

A DOG'S TAIL

and lucky for me I smelled some not too far away from my home, as it turned out.

Actually, it was *super* close. I ended up back at my house where I belonged!

But then I got put back into the kennel.

But that's okay because now I know how to make it out of this place! For good!

Yeah, this was my home earlier but now I'm going solo. I'm gonna strike out on my own!

Okay so it's the same plan as before: ring the bell to go to the bathroom and then slip out of my collar. Let's try it out!

It has worked again! Now I just need to find... wait, what's that smell?

It's food and I seem to be going in its path!?!?

Yet again I come inside and am in the kennel (boo-hoo).

I don't know how they tricked me like that.

Anyway. At least I got the food.

A DOG'S TAIL

People

People (*people* people, not dog people) are odd strange creatures. They speak all sorts of different words yet they don't understand me.

Like the time I was outside. I was trying to tell the people to let me out — out of the yard — but they looked at me like I was crazy. You know who are the crazy ones? Them!

A DOG'S TAIL

I've tried all the languages I know: French Poodle, **German Shepherd**, and even **Mutt**. But guess what? None of them worked!

People!

I guess it's not their fault they're kinda dumb.

Wild Side

Now you probably know me by now as a nice, calm, sweet guy. But did you know there was another side of me? It emerges when my dad comes out of his den from watching TV or whatever to play with me.

It gets me in touch with the wild.

Just imagine it — in the house, I'm hiding behind a couch, cleverly eluding capture, when, suddenly, I smell... a hunter!

He jumps out! And, discretion being the better part of valor...

...I flee.

But it's harder than it sounds! They've set booby traps all around the house to catch me off guard — like the falling phone chargers, and the dancing floor lamps that insist in getting in the way. It's like running a gauntlet!

Here's another one. Say, for instance, you are playing monkey-in-the-middle, as my humans like to call it.

(For some reason, apparently, they can't tell the difference between a monkey and a dog. I pity them sometimes.)

Anyway, before I so rudely interrupted myself, the objective is to get the toy (which is usually a ball).

It's harder than you'd think, though. Dad throws it over my head and my sister catches it. Then she does the same, throwing it back to him.

And they laugh because I can't reach it with my ~~short~~ sturdy little legs.

Again, a lot of fun... **NOT**. But don't you worry — I will make my displeasure known. Just wait.

A DOG'S TAIL

Who's the Bully?

I have met these two birds called Pip and Peep. They are little chicks that came from a hen. They say they were raised on a farm. But we live in the suburbs!

Their mom must have had a problem with keeping track of the birdies in the nest and, I hate to say, that she didn't teach them proper stuff about the way the world works. Like, for instance, they aren't afraid of me *and yet they should be!* After all...

Who's the dog here!?!?

Right? I mean, am I right or am I right?

Anyway, I am always looking forward to seeing them because that gets me one step closer to eating them. But, they are so annoying that I never really end up getting a chance!

Okay, I know what you're thinking. You're thinking all like, *"But why would you want to eat something so cute and innocent?!"* You know. In that ridiculous voice you people use.

Well, if hamburgers were all cute and innocent... okay, just pretend... so if hamburgers were all cute and innocent, right, then why would you eat them? Why would you want to eat them?

See? It's called logic.

On the other hand, I love hamburgers too, myself. So maybe hamburgers aren't really the best example to use. But still. You get the idea.

A DOG'S TAIL

Are You Leaving?

Even though I'm absolutely perfectly well-behaved, my owners leave me all alone in the house. Okay, in the... the... the kennel!

Sometimes they don't put me in my kennel. Sometimes they take me with them. But, that's usually to the vet! One time I had to get 4 shots and those shots felt like bullets!

A DOG'S TAIL

I'm not even kidding. Like 4 bullets.
Blam! Blam! Blam! Blam!
Like that.
You wouldn't have liked it either, believe me.

Owner Sick

If your family goes on vacation without you, you know how I feel.

So this one time, I was left in a prison yard (or what they call "dog boarding"), while my so-called "family" went far away on a trip for skiing.

Well, so I had a plan to bring the fleet of butlers back to me (see, there's an evil side of me).

A DOG'S TAIL

I decided to act like I was sick. Then, hearing that I was sick, they would rush back to get me!

My plan couldn't fail!

Mwa-ha-ha.

The hard part was that I had to resist the temptation of food that was offered by the warden (who was quite rude and doesn't like me talking to the other prisoners — but, clearly, I don't like talking, right?). So I had to stay in my kennel and avoid food.

But my plan worked and soon enough my ~~butlers~~ family came back.

Boy was I happy! So happy I might have done a flip!

(If I wasn't pretending to be sick, that is).

(And if I could do flips.)

A DOG'S TAIL

A High Percent of Showers

I hate water! Especially once it's being poured over me.

So this one time, one of my owners put a leash on me and I was like, "Yeah, alright, I needed a walk, let's go, sister."

But she really put the leash on tight to make sure I didn't go out of her sight, so that she could get me into the bathroom. Once I saw the

A DOG'S TAIL

tub I was a little confused but was like, "Well, okay, first I'll get a drink and then we'll go on our walk. That's cool."

Turned out she got what she wanted — for me to take a bath — while I got what I didn't want: a high percent of showers.

NOT cool!

A Wild Feast

Have you ever wondered, *"Matchi, how did you get so fat, anyway?"* Okay, well, first, I'm gonna ignore the rudeness of that question.

But, yeah. Funny story. See, even though I've eaten a lot of leftovers, that wasn't enough for me. So I started to catch game for myself. Then, I would take it to the rain water in the sandpit and clean

A DOG'S TAIL

it off (so that there is no blood on it — though sometimes it does make a good soup).

So then I'd eat all the game I caught.

And that's the story of how I got so fat.

I'm Tired

Once I go on walks, we always end up probably running a whole mile. Probably more. Probably lots more.

Once we get home, I slurp up all the water in my water bowl.

I get so tired that I go on cold tile to cool myself down. There I lay, sticking my tongue out on the tile floor and slowly falling asleep...

A DOG'S TAIL

while my owners eat dinner without me!

That's right, sometimes life isn't hardly very fair.

Mattress Mining

Now I sleep on my owner's bed with them. But, I haven't been doing too well on the "not-ripping-up-the-bed" part.

You see, it all started when I was playing a game. People were chasing me around the house. I got so scared that I started digging a hole in the mattress to escape.

It was working, too!

But I didn't see dirt.

A DOG'S TAIL

I did see a few angry owners, though, and these little tiny white pellet things I call mice (because they look like mice).

I made the excuse that I was trying to make the mattress covers look nice, even though I ripped them a little.

I got put in the kennel anyway.
(Okay so I ripped them a lot.)
(But still.)

You Wanna Fight, Short-Pants?

I was outside on the lawn minding my own business while doing my business when a little chihuahua started barking like crazy at me.

That little chihuahua might have been small but he jumped the outer gate while dragging his owner behind him!

I was all like, "So you wanna fight, short-pants?!" You know.

A DOG'S TAIL

Ready to go and do some damage, right?

But the owner finally got a grip and tugged that dog free. That chihuahua would have faced my wrath, though. You know he woulda.

He's lucky, that's for sure.

Now whenever I go out in the yard, I wait for Lil' Spoiled Pup.

Ms. Annoying-Pants

I was watching for anything unusual once, and I saw a cat! She was black and mean.

I barked, "Hello!" but she turned her back. Rude, I know.

That made me mad. I kept on barking and howling. She ignored me even though she could hear me just fine.

A DOG'S TAIL

So then I tell her to get off my property and scare her, but she didn't listen.

She never listens. She just sits there. Ridiculous, I know. She is so annoying I could... I could break the fence!

Wait, that gives me an idea...

Doses of Poison

One day I woke up to an itch. I also had war scars on my fur. My owners sent me to the vet. The vet gave us medicine, or, in my case ☠ **poison** ☠, to make me better.

I quickly learned that medicine tastes bad and so I figured out that not taking the medication is better than taking the medication — obviously. Right?

A DOG'S TAIL

They thought they could trick me by sticking the poison — I mean pills — in hot dogs and... well, I can't resist hot dogs.

So I just started eating around the pill, so I only ate hotdog, and I left the pill (mixed with half-eaten hotdog mush & saliva, for visual effect) on the floor for them to find.

That mess-stain would remind them of what happened the day they tried to fool me into eating poison. This will be a valuable lesson for them.

Who is That??!!

I was playing outside and noticed someone was mocking me. By "someone" I mean another dog.

Anyway, once I barked, he barked. Once I stopped barking, he stopped barking.

At first I thought it was coincidental but after a while it still didn't stop. So I told him, "Come out and show yourself, if you're not a coward."

A DOG'S TAIL

All he said back was, "Come out and show yourself, if you're not a coward."

I said, **"I'm not a coward! YOU'RE a coward!"**

Every night I think about him, and what he might look like, and if he'll come and face me, or if he'll be a dumb coward forever.

Mine!

While my family is at the dinner table, sometimes they'll slip me some food, drop food on the floor by accident, or I just get leftovers afterwards.

Yum!

I like leftovers the most because I get a lot of food that way. Either way, anything on the floor (or anything I can reach when they're

A DOG'S TAIL

not looking or paying attention) is mine!

Scat Exploration

Once we go on a walk, that's my scat-exploration time! Okay, so I'll tell you how it's done. With a little practice, maybe you'll be able to do it too.

First, while you're out walking, concentrate on finding some scat.

Then, sniff around carefully for the scat to catch its scent.

Finally, follow the scent to get...

💩 **Your Prize** 💩

A DOG'S TAIL

I have to warn you, though — it is tricky to master. I took two dog years to master it myself.

Anyhow, this one time, I was in my scat-exploration mode —deep in *the zone*, you know? — and, unexpectedly, I got the scent of the Lil' Spoiled Pup himself!

I begged my owner to go but he wouldn't. This happens all the time (them not doing what I want) ☹

Secret Spy Hideouts

Once I do something I know is gonna get me in trouble, I have secret hideouts in the house. They keep me hidden from my owners. Then, sometimes, I don't end up getting in trouble because once they see my irresistible face they can't resist!

The hiding spots are under the bed, closets & pantries, and also sleeping under a blanket.

A DOG'S TAIL

I have a 30%–40% chance of this working. The rest of the 60%–70% is that I get caught.

Bugged by Ticks

Me and my family went on a camping trip. We would wake up in the middle of the night because they thought their beds had bedbugs in them.

Once we got home, we had to inspect everybody for bedbugs and ticks. But I wasn't inspected — *me*, the most important person!

A few weeks went by while I was itching like crazy. I was inspected —

A DOG'S TAIL

finally — and they found a deer tick.

Good thing they got it and killed it cause I would've ended up itching my head off.

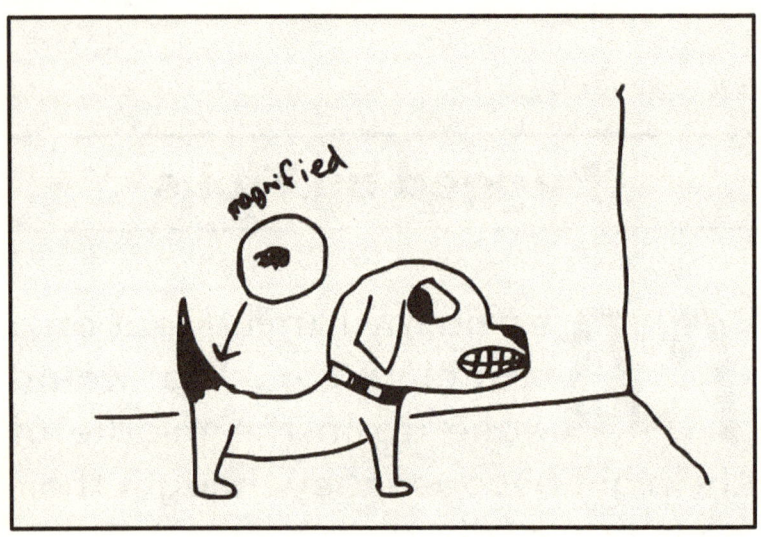

Rules of Engagement

So, earlier, I was playing with my family and everything was fine at first... but then something smelt fishy — and not the good kind of fishy (slurp), either.

See, once we started playing, the thing was, they didn't use the rules of engagement!

That's right. There are rules to these things. Proper etiquette must be maintained! And they didn't

A DOG'S TAIL

follow the first part: which is don't cuddle or pet me (this might seem strange to you, but there's a proper time and place for cuddling and petting).

And that's not all. To play, I hold the rope and you (the human) come fetch it. Then, I will come and try to take it away. Once I get ahold of it, you must pull as hard as you can! It's simple.

The rules are simple!

But do they ever learn? No. No, they don't.

Matchi Mansion

Today my human sister is very excited. Okay, first, I should say that my sister is my favorite of my pack. Don't tell the others, though, okay? It might make them sad and you gotta remember that humans have feelings too even though they're humans.

Anyway so a girl walked in to play with my sister, while the girl's

A DOG'S TAIL

mother went in the other room and talked with Mom.

I walked over to introduce myself to my sister's friend, and right away she said she loved me. Of course, I get this all the time. Remember I told you about my irresistible face?

After they had dinner, they played and watched TV. We woke up this morning and ate breakfast. Then we had the walk. A little bit after the walk, they showed me the:

Matchi Mansion

Now I don't know just yet if this Matchi Mansion is a good or a bad thing, but, so far... I'm not loving it.

I guess it's not totally their fault, though. After all, there's no way anyone can turn a basement into a place nice enough that it's fit for someone as sophisticated as me.

What I mean is, it's not their fault that they're human and so don't always know how to run a dog joint properly.

You've just got to remember that their hearts are — usually, at least — in the right place.

A DOG'S TAIL

I Could Use Some Help

I was bored and tired of sitting at home this one day. Once my father saw me, he was a little worried so he gave me a **KONG WOBBLER**™. It smelled like hot dogs. I love hotdogs, like I said before.

There was a hole on the **KONG WOBBLER**. I scratched, clawed, scraped, and asked the humans about it. I damaged it, I think... but **KONG** popped back up unharmed.

My dad decided to make it a little easier for me (even though I'd just about gotten it). So I tried my dad's way. And then I tried *my* version of my dad's way (I just used my mouth instead of my paws).

My dad and sister watched me until my sister took it away.

WWWHHHYYY! *I was so close.*

She gave it to our dad.

Puh-lease don't put me in the kennel.

But I'd gotten worried for nothing because Dad showed me the **KONG WOBBLER** and then took off the cap. He finally — I don't think anyone has ever done this — just *gave* the hot dog to me!

A few years after that, they got the **KONG WOBBLER** out again. *This time I'm going to get it!* is what I said, because I still remembered that **KONG** *WOBBLER*, and the trick my dad showed me.

So this time I held the **KONG** *WOBBLER* in between my paws and used my mouth to screw the lid off.

Ta-da!

Then I did a happy dance that went like this:

🎵 *I did it, uh-huh,*
You didn't, oh-yeah 🎶

A DOG'S TAIL

The Food Frightening Dreams

One day, while the rest of the family was out of the house, my sister watched me for a bit. She took a seat and started playing piano.

I was tired and the calm music was making me sleepy. I laid down and slowly fell asleep.

I started dreaming that I was in a **Food Wonderland!** The best part was that everything was puppy-friendly! I could eat and chew anything I wanted.

But, then, while swimming (and slurping) in the yogurt pool, I felt a rumble and a thump.

Thump! THUMP!

I slowly turned my head.

ROAR! A giant monster made out of hamburgers!

Mmmmm, hamburgers!

Naturally, I did what any dog would do...

Owwhhhh! Owwhhhh! The food-o-monster got angrier.

Dumb monster! It's not *my* fault you're delicious!

Then he started destroying everything. But I figured, hey, he *is* made out of food. I can just *eat* him, and too bad if he didn't like it, right?

So I started eating him.

I wasn't even halfway done when my sister woke me up. Turns out I was making weird noises while I was asleep. They were high-pitched and sounded like I was crying. Oh, well!

A DOG'S TAIL

The Bunnies Did It!

It was just starting to become spring and my sister began mentioning about making a *garden*.

In a few weeks, the plants started popping up and sprouting. Soon I could see a tall tomato plant towering above me.

Then I thought, "If this garden thing has anything to do with food, then I'm all in! Maybe the next time

A DOG'S TAIL

I need to go out (to use the bathroom), I can get some of these 'plants' and eat them."

But when I looked at the cherry tree, it was too young and thin to support the weight of a dog.

So no cherries.

I know that humans use tomatoes all the time in cooking. But the tomato plant was too tall for me to reach.

But I've started to smell a strong scent of bunnies. And where there's bunnies, there's carrots. So I started digging where the bunny scent was strong. I found these things stuck in the ground. They were oddly-shaped but, frankly, tasted just like carrots.

I ate all of the carrot-tasting things (that turned out to be carrots, actually).

Yay for me!

When my owners found out about it, they thought it was the bunnies that did it. And I was like, "Yup! It was the bunnies alright!"

After a month or two (in human years), they felt like maybe it wasn't the bunnies after all. They felt like it was me!

Luckily I'm just a dog so how am I supposed to know that I'm not allowed to go stealing people's food outside?

I mean, first, they don't let me do it inside and, now, apparently, they aren't gonna let me steal people's food outside either??

Whatever!

I'll just blame it on the bunnies.

A DOG'S TAIL

A Sweet Treat

One day, my sister and father decided to grab some coffee (it's a human thing) but I couldn't let them leave. Why couldn't I let them leave? Because I couldn't let them leave, I just said!

Anyway, they settled on letting me come but that my sister would have to hold me so that I wouldn't run away while my dad was

A DOG'S TAIL

grabbing cake pops and coffee (that's what he said, anyway).

We got in the car and had fun on the ride to Starbucks. Once there, my dad got into a line with other cars and then started talking to a little box on a pole.

I know. It's weird what humans do sometimes, right?

(Before I tell you the next part, you must listen. I always howl at people or dogs. It's my thing, okay? It's what I do Anyways, back to the story.)

My father told my sister, *"Hold Matchi!"* So she grabbed my leash and held on for dear life.

Once we go around a little turn, my dad opens the window. I start howling because I see a lady giving my dad food.

The lady notices me and says, *"Hold on,"* and then she comes back with a lid with whipped cream all on it.

For me!

It was very thoughtful for her to give that to me. I have to admit, some humans do share and care.

A DOG'S TAIL

I See You

Some days, when most of my pack is out hunting whatever it is that humans hunt (coffee, mostly, it seems) when they could be (and should be) playing with me instead, I take that time to look at my friends around the house — the stuffed animals!

I look at them and think, "I'll just take their eyes out a little bit,

A DOG'S TAIL

along with the nose." Guess what, they even agree with me ... I think.

I've done this before and their noses taste like gummy bears, while the eyes are like gobstoppers.

Anyway, I was about to start the fun once again until the party-poopers came back home and ruined the day, taking away all the fun I'd planned.

(boo-hoo)

Not cool ☹

Aim 'n' ... Fire!

My owners had put some grass seed down and I sort of, well... killed it.

But I must kill the new seeds! How else will I go??

See, if there is a good patch of grass, I'm going to have to pee in it for at least 10 days. And I get a sense of relief. It sure feels good.

But it also gives the grass a nice color. So I try to decorate the

A DOG'S TAIL

grass with the pretty yellow color that also flattens the grass to make it nice and smooth.

I am an artist!

I could try doing designs, too, but that would be too much work and would probably cut into my important eating time anyway.

But, anyway, so my owners can add their plants and flowers to the yard but I shouldn't pee?!

It hardly seems fair.

Gas Engine

I have a skill that helps me conquer my arch-nemesis, my arch-nemesis being... stairs!

I know you might think that birds are my nemesis, or squirrels, but none of them are more annoying than stairs!

But sometimes I can cheat. You see, I use gas to do this and it helps a lot, though I am only able to use my glorious farting superpower once a day.

Yesterday, I was able to do all 13 stairs in 7 farts. But, today, I did it in 4!

I'm trying to bring it down to 1.

It helps if you're very fat. See, the fatter you are, the more farts you can generate.

Too bad I'm not!

A DOG'S TAIL

The Fun Prison

My family is going on vacation. Yay! But are leaving me behind. Boo-hoo.

But I do get to meet my friends. They are also dogs — who have been neglected, but they get to party. So I get to join in.

It's going to be awesome! So I packed everything.

🐾 Towel?

Check!

🐾 Ropie?

The 2nd check!

🐾 Food?

Check!

All ready! I packed everything!

(Huh? What do you mean my *owners* packed everything? Well, okay, but I supervised and that's the most important part!)

It is so much fun to go there, you get to eat, sleep, and play, and... actually, now that I think about it, the only differences are that you sleep in a cell and get fed less food.

Hmmm.

The only good part is that I get to meet my friends, and get to party with them. Eh, I guess it isn't that bad.

A DOG'S TAIL

Oh wait, I remember, I also get to bark all I want!

Also, I can't bring this book along. Otherwise, what will the other dogs think of me?

A DOG'S TAIL

Cat in My Throat

Sorry, hang on — *i COUGH i i COUGH i* — came home with a scratchy, dry throat.

What?!? You think, from all that barking at prison, it caused my throat to turn dry? Puh-lease, I would have been better by now.

WHAT?! You think it would've taken at least a day? Honestly, us dogs are stronger than humans. Take my word for it.

That means that all sources lead to a cat?

WHAT THE WHAA—??! You think cats are harmless creatures?

I can't stand you anymore, close this book right now and think about what you said. That didn't just hurt me in my throat, it hurt me in my heart. **In my HEART** ♥

A DOG'S TAIL

Guardian of the Peaches

Once I am outside, I have 1 duty... well, okay, 2 duties. Okay, so 1 doody and 1 duty. After my doody duty, my other one besides that is guarding the peaches.

That is why I go out of the house so often. Plus, I need the fresh air.

You see, when I'm not outside, animals and creatures (of the non-dog variety) will come into my backyard and eat (basically) my peaches off (basically) my peach tree (basically)!

I worked so hard on testing the taste of them...

(Mmmm)

... and making sure the dirt is fertile, and watering (basically) my peach tree.

My family comes out and helps me pick them and we all get to eat them.

(Mmmm again!)

A DOG'S TAIL

Acid Rain

Do you want to know how I water the garden? Well too bad if you don't.

So it works like this. First, I ring the bell to go outside. Then, I go outside. I must stay alert for squirrels, birds, and bunnies, so they can't get in the yard. I must also water the plants.

What do you mean dogs can't water plants?? They so can. Plus, I

A DOG'S TAIL

do it all the time. I also make sure to water the grass.

What do you mean, *"Oh, now I get how"?* Okay, let me just tell you a story...

Long ago, when fire hydrants were invented, the only way to fill them up was with a dog. Dogs would pee on the fire hydrants to fill them up. Fast-forward to today, I know that fire hydrants have water inside and they are getting water from dog pee and plants need water, right? So each day when I go out to pee, I do it on the evergreen trees.

(That wasn't supposed to rhyme or anything, so don't even.)

A DOG'S TAIL

Weed Feed

I love going on walks to get my inner dog spirit out. It helps out with the stressful schedule I have.

I mean, okay, so I have to eat, then play, then sleep, then eat, and then eat some more! Plus, after all that, I'm also a happiness helper!

Anyway so I have a busy life. You get it, right? Right.

A DOG'S TAIL

I also love running, so when the little girl (my human sister, like I keep telling you, if only you'd pay attention!) offers me to run, I always accept.

We go running down the sidewalk but, eventually, we stop. We stop for a break, that is... and then do it again!

We do it one last time after crossing the bridge and then we slow down and walk. This is my favorite part of the route because we get to — I mean *I* get to — eat white fluffy weeds.

What? Why would I eat weeds? Easy! They give me a boost, they're delicious, and sometimes they have water inside which helps a lot too!

Sure, they aren't the best thing in the world for dogs to eat, probably — but it sure beats

nothing! They do however, have a dry aftertaste.
    shrugs
    Oh, well.

A DOG'S TAIL

Limbo!

Everyone will agree that I love food because that is how my owners taught me my first move... **SIT!**

But now I can do anything with a piece of food. By that I mean, if food is the prize, then I've got it covered.

So, today, I am pretty sure they decided to teach me the limbo. They've got this stick set up out in

A DOG'S TAIL

the yard, parallel with the ground, so I figure it's gotta be limbo, right?

Then they say something like "dump" or "gump" — it's hard to tell because humans don't speak clearly like dogs do — and then I crawl under the stick.

Perfect every time! See? I told you I was good at this stuff.

Hang on, what? What, you think they want me to go *over* the stick? Please. I've been in this house way longer than you. So, trust me, I know stuff — and what you're saying doesn't even make sense because this is definitely limbo we're playing.

Anyway, like I was gonna say before I was so rudely interrupted, the strange thing is that they aren't even giving me food when I walk over to the other side perfect every time like I just said.

What? What do you mean, *"Ha! See? I was right!"* You're not even making any sense again. But in a weird way you are, I guess, because I tried it your way just this once and the craziest thing is that I ended up getting the treat for no reason at all. *At all.*

Humans are definitely weird sometimes.

A DOG'S TAIL

The Change in Diet

Lately, I've been changing my diet. As you know (if you've been paying attention), I am forced to eat dry, tasteless kibble pretty much every day!

I do not care for kibble. So I have devised a plan and, if I play my cards right, it should work brilliantly.

You're probably wondering how this plan works. It is simple: I sit in the corner while I wait for food. They then place the kibble in my food bowl. Then they say, "Release!" (like they always do — don't ask me why).

But, of course I don't go. Then they realize what I want — I want food (**REAL** food). And so they go to the fridge and FAKE getting it, like, rattling around jars and stuff to make me THINK they're getting me real food (even though they're not).

Any normal dog might very well fall for this trick but you have to remember something important:

I am not a normal dog.

Right, so I remain keen and sharp (this being a war of wits, after all), waiting for the "human touch" in my food.

Finally, they give in and let me get the smell of the treat (to show me it's really real) and then they put it in my dish.

And this, my friends, is the quick and easy way to get the human touch.

A DOG'S TAIL

Taxi!

I may seem like a dog who's exceptionally fit, handsome, and intelligent (all true, of course), but, believe it or not, I don't always like running.

And today just so happened to be one of those days. One of my owners did some warm-ups with me to get me ready. Thanks a lot (*SARCASM*), because instead of going my regular one mile, I would only have enough energy to go half of that. Anyway, when we go for a run, I must always be in front and I must run all the way until I have run almost a mile. Then I normally run out of gas and lay on the ground and bark, **"Taxi!"**

But of course, there *has* to be a language barrier because the taxi NEVER ARRIVES!

So I look up at the big guy (my pack leader, or so he thinks) with a face that says *can-you-give-me-a-piggyback-ride-please?*

And he picks me up off the ground and lets me hang my tongue out as he carries me. Later, after I'm all rested up, he puts me back down.

Then I run the rest of the way back home!

My sister has picked me up, too... *once.*

She's little and I'm probably too fat (I mean **muscular!**) for her to lift. She probably thought, *"Oh, man, this dog is WAY too muscular for me to carry again."*

Yup. I'm sure that's what she musta thought.

A DOG'S TAIL

What a Shocker

Help me! A dark and evil wizard is doing some magic on me!

You see, when he gets bored he goes to his magic crystal ball and tortures me. That reminds me...

I love balls.

Sorry, now where was I? Oh, yeah. The wizard. He electrocutes me whenever he pleases. It's so annoying.

A DOG'S TAIL

I've never seen this wizard but I have to assume he exists because who *else* but an evil wizard could be electrocuting me?

In completely unrelated news, I just got a new collar. It's super cool, with a small box on it. I really don't know what the little metal box does. But, of course, I know what I *want* it to do.

What, I'm so predictable that you know exactly what I'm going to say? Oh, yeah? Prove it!

Now where was I? Oh, yeah. The box and what I want it to do. Well, I want it to contain **food** inside the little box is what I want it to do.

One day, the wizard took it up a notch by making the zapping hurt a whole lot more.

My owners took the collar off this morning and, coincidentally, I haven't encountered the wizard since. But something tells me I may confront him yet again, and next time he may not back down. Well what he doesn't know is that I don't give up!

Wait, do you smell that? I just caught the scent of something. It's a... it's a squirrel!

Okay-gotta-go-bye!

A DOG'S TAIL

Bunnies Are Buddies

Ahhhhhh! Answering the call of nature makes me feel sooooo much better.

Wait, did I just miss a bunny-rabbit? *I did!?*

I'm telling you, I didn't see or smell him/her!

I was a little busy just now and got distracted. It happens!

But, oh, man, if the other dogs catch wind of this they will definitely put me to shame. I'll never hear the end of it!

This is horrible, I'll be the laughing stock of the neighborhood!

The only way to make sure I don't become the laughing stock is to catch a bunny-rabbit.

Look over there, I see one.

Lemme at him.

Wait, my owners are watching.

Hmmm, laughing stock or face a long stick? Well, laughing stock is way better than facing a stick. But...

...I need to talk to this bunny.

"Hey, Mr. Bunny-Rabbit. Let me make you a deal."

Mr. Bunny-Rabbit twitched his nose. It looked like was bracing himself, all ready to run away real fast if things turned bad quickly. But Mr. Bunny-Rabbit didn't know that my intentions here were only good intentions.

"You see, if you let me become your buddy, then I will never try to scare or eat a bunny-rabbit ever again."

And that is the true story of how bunnies became buddies.

A DOG'S TAIL

Drag Racing

I am a dog-renowned drag racer. Didn't you know that? Yeah, well there's a lot of things you didn't know about me.

But now is not the time to tell you about all those other things. Now is the time to tell you about this one specific thing.

You see, drag racing is a well-known sport in the dog community. And the puppies with more leg-

A DOG'S TAIL

power are generally the better drag racers (and you'll soon see why).

How do you play the game, you say? Great question, Jimmy.

What? That's not your name? Wow! I'm usually pretty good with names.

Anyway, all you need for this sport is one human, a dog, a collar, and a leash. Easy-peasy, lemon-squeezy.

Got it? Great!

Now I am only going to say this once, so listen closely: The dog must wear the collar with the leash clipped on. The human holds the leash. Then, the dog drags the human behind him by running as fast as possible!

I am the fastest drag-racer around. So if you think you're up to the challenge, go ahead and find me and ...

The race is on!

A DOG'S TAIL

Take Me Out for a Run

Do you know that human song that goes something like:

♫ *Take me out to the ball game,* ♪
♫ *Take me out to the, la-la-la, whatever* ♪♪

...that one?

A DOG'S TAIL

Yeah well that's how I feel when I want to go on a walk or run. It's so much fun!

(Unless I'm not in the mood to run — but we're talking now about the times that I am, obviously.)

Do you remember when I told you about how they leave me at home? Well I found a way to tell them, *"Take me with you, please."*

Would you like to know? Well too bad if you don't because I'm gonna tell you anyway.

I have collected some data (dogs are good at Science, if you didn't know) and I have realized that humans need these things called "shoes" (which also happen to taste pretty good, by the way).

Now, as per my meticulous analysis of the collected *"shoe"* data, I've determined that they are needed for humans to go outside. Plus, there are two of each.

(Now, as to *why* humans need shoes in order to go outside, well, that is outside the scope of the current study and will perhaps be examined at a later date.)

Presently, I have what human people call a "plan" — and it has formed somewhere in the cranial region of my brain.

This is my plan: All I have to do is what human people call implementing. Do you want to hear it? Well too bad if you don't because, again, I'm going to tell you anyway.

This is important!

It's SCIENCE!

Right, so what I will do is steal someone's shoe. Then I run around

A DOG'S TAIL

the house with it, and give it back to them...

...but **only** once they've given me their guarantee of time for me to go outside.

🐕 **Dogs are clever people** 🐕

Yawn

Sometimes people do boring things that, somehow, they still think are fun. Every time I try to play as well, though, I don't have all that much fun.

One of these boring human games is when all you do is move little pieces across the board. How much more boring can that get??

And I've tried playing, but it's too hard for a dog like me. So I like to jazz it up a little by picking up my

A DOG'S TAIL

rope and trying to get their attention with it. But even that is hard because they're usually concentrating on those little pieces on the board too much to pay proper attention to me like they know they should be doing.

When they finish (after, like, the 12th of never), they'll usually **finally** play something I can play — knowing I've been yawning my head off.

A Slice of Paradise

Do you know those ads about buying a slice of paradise, as they call it? Well that's not what this is about.

This is about how during walks & runs I stay **strong**.

You see, we walk for a very long time and I really need water but my owners don't think about water. Or they think I won't need water or something and don't bring it.

I mean, humans being humans, who knows *what* they actually think about — *if* they even think at all??

(I mean proper thinking, like dogs do.)

And oh sure that is completely **FINE BY ME!**

Sorry to yell.

So what do I do, you ask? Great question, Billy! Halfway into my walks, I stop at an island that I discovered. I call this wonderful island *dun du-du-dun*...

Water Island

(It's a clever name. You don't have to tell me — I already know.)

So what do I do there, you say? Great question, Sammy!

I...

..Drink...

....Water!

It's my slice of paradise.

A DOG'S TAIL

A Close Encounter

It was a dark, warm night. As I went outside for the night shift, I felt like I was being watched — and not just by my mom.

I saw a shadow in the night. It was like a dog, but bigger. Like bigger than a golden retriever. Those golden retrievers, they think they are just **soooo** perfect.

AHEM Sorry.

Now where was I?

A DOG'S TAIL

It was a big shadowy night-creature. A big **DARK** shadowy night-creature. The creature was hairy and flea-bitten.

(How do I know it was flea-bitten? I just do!)

I wanted to scream but I couldn't.

I gulped ⊃ *gulp*

What *was* this alien creature?
What did it *want* from me??
Why is it here???

(If I die, I hope someone sees this writing because it'll be the last thing I ever said right before the dying part ((unless maybe I was to say something really quick — and I mean *really* quick)) right directly after this.)

Just when I thought I would become chopped liver (and not the good kind), I heard a familiar voice calling me inside.

I sprinted up the steps and safely back into my home.

And, oh, so it turns out that the creature was a **COYOTE**. If I'd stayed out there any longer, I would've been in his tummy right now!!

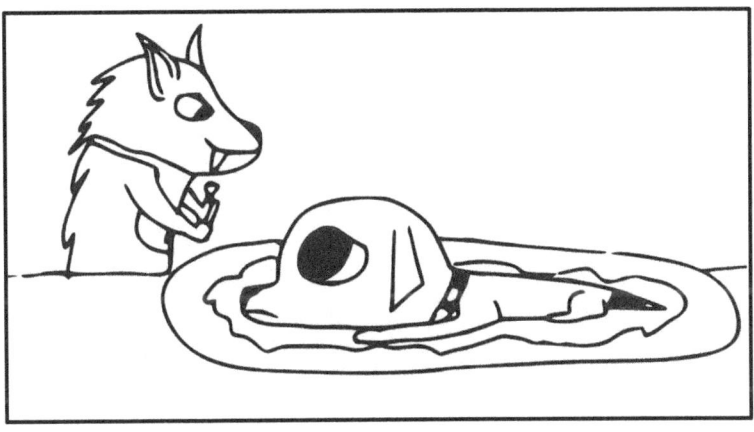

A DOG'S TAIL

Own the Throne

As I was performing my regular neighborhood watch duties, I spotted some lampposts. Now, you're probably wondering, *"What does a lamppost have to do with a dog?"*

Well when lampposts were invented, they would routinely burn out — a very inefficient system. But recent dog studies have shown that, following the switch to ecologically-friendly dog-urine power, 68 out of

A DOG'S TAIL

100 lamp posts have exhibited marked signs of improvement. So, now, once every dog hits 21 years of age (in dog years), they must find an unclaimed lamppost and claim it as their own (and keep it powered up).

Anyway, I sniff this one lamppost and guess who peed there? Short-Pants!

The next one was taken by... a **PIT BULL?!**

Sorry. I thought not having food was scary but just the mere thought of a... **PIT BULL—!!!**

Sorry again. Anyhow, there are only 2 more lampposts left to check. Alright, so this one is taken by... the one and (okay, maybe not) only *Ms. Annoying-Pants?!* Oh, I forgot. She's a stray cat. Okay, I'll let this one slide.

And now the final one is taken by... well, okay, now *me*.

I'm so happy! I'm so happy I could do the **Cha-Cha Slide!**

You see, if I hadn't done it — if I hadn't found a lamppost of my very own to tend to — I'd be put to shame by all the other dogs. They'd laugh at me more than the dog who couldn't spot a bunny that was right behind him.

Glad I'm not *him* *COUGH*

A DOG'S TAIL

My Schooling

Guess what? Last week I graduated! What, you don't think dogs go to college? Well they do!

Anyway, I graduated Howled University with a *Beagle Cum Loude* degree (that's Latin for *Beagle With Loud Distinction*). That is a very hard school to get into, so lemme tell ya, I was really excited to get the acceptance bark.

A DOG'S TAIL

The test was very difficult to pass. Your barking form must be perfect, with grace and movement. Your sound must be loud and ear-splitting. And you must be able to move corner-to-corner in a simulated household room swiftly and accurately.

Also, your begging must be cute and get you a treat (at least that part was easy — adorable face, remember?).

I know what you're thinking: *"All that work to graduate? That's a lot!"* But only a smart, handsome, clever, funny dog like me will only ever be a graduate from Howled University.

Which is as it should be.

Howling (Basic)	Howling (Movement)
Begging	Growling

A DOG'S TAIL

Top Dog

You probably didn't know that I am an amazing actor. It all started when I played The Wolf in *Little Red Riding Hood*. And that was where my acting career began.

Then I played the Big Bad Wolf in *The Three Little Pigs*. Years later, when a reboot of the Three Little Pigs franchise was in the works, I was hired — this time as one of the

A DOG'S TAIL

Pigs (my agent didn't want me to be typecast).

Like I said, I was supposed to play one of the Pigs, but, when I came on set, they said I was too "attached" to my old costume. They told me I had to ditch the canine look, otherwise they were gonna give the part to someone else.

Anyway, the director ended up getting mad at me and firing me but then I said, **"You can't fire me because I *QUIT!*"**

I loved acting. I was a star and that director blew it for me. Ah, well. It was a good run while it lasted.

I guess that's ✪SHOWBIZ✪ !

A DOG'S TAIL

There's a Pit Bull on the Loose

HELP ME! HELP ME! I saw the pit bull! He was walking so casually, so calm, and all peaceful and stuff. Almost like he wasn't a monster!

Until he saw me, of course. And then we both wanted to fight so badly, so badly that I made a song about it and here it goes right now...

A DOG'S TAIL

♫ *There's a pit bull on the loose,* ♪
there's a pit bull on the loose.
I gotta take him down,
otherwise I'm gonna lose.
♫ *And if I do lose,*
and if I do lose,
I will be hurt,
There is no excuse! ♪♪

Birthday Bash

Today was very weird. Everyone has been acting strangely.

I mean, yes, it's my birthday and all. But usually I just always get a happy-birthday song and that's that. But as if I weren't weirded out enough already today, then what happened next was beyond odd.

When my sister came home, instead of giving me my treat like usual, she started talking to my dad. Then, he pulled out a HUGE

A DOG'S TAIL

package. I sniffed it a little and, not smelling any food inside, was about to walk away and carry on with my day.

But then my sister started to open the package and untie the ribbon and everything.

I wasn't too excited about the basket until I looked inside. There were dog toys and treats and collars and leashes.

So it all turned out all right in the end.

Small Spaces

I have a dark secret. I am claustrophobic. I know that I am the smart, handsome, perfect dog that you've come to know, but, seriously, this is a real problem for me.

It all started when I was put in the kennel for the first time and no one was in the house.

I saw this long skinny thing swishing around suspiciously. My

first instinctive reaction, of course, as anyone's would be, was...
SNAAKEE!
EVERYBODY RUN FOR YOUR LIVES!"

But then I mustered up my courage, because Matchi is nothing if not courageous. After all, I thought, Matchi is so very big (and courageous) and this snake is so very small. And so it doesn't stand a chance.

I started attacking it!

Well, the funny thing is, I thought I could easily just crush the vile creature in my massive, powerful jaws, right? But...

Every time I bit the snake, it bit me back in the tail at exactly the same time! How did it do that??

Its scales started falling off with each chomp and yank I gave it.

I thought that it must hurt, but, strangely, it seemed fine.

It was swishing around more than ever!

Finally, my humans came and let me out of the death cage. But instead of the warm, loving arms I was expecting, they all just stood there with horrified looks on their funny human faces.

They were looking at my tail.

I saw it, too.

MY TAIL HAD BEEN CHEWED ON BY THE SNAKE!

But...

...my tail was suddenly looking a whole lot like the snake.

What the what??

A DOG'S TAIL

Okay so it turned out there was no snake in my kennel after all, but there *was* a large amount of fur.

Whoops-a-daisy.

But, lucky me, my tail fur has grown back. So the story has a happy ending.

Yay!

Surprise Attack

Today was weird. My brother was staying in his room too much and NOT PLAYING WITH ME!!
AT ALL!!
Ridiculous, right?
But, I came up with a plan.
A good plan.
A very good plan.
A very, very, good plan.

A DOG'S TAIL

Oh, what, you wanna know what it is? Well why didn't you say so??

Okay, so to illustrate my ingenious plan, have a look at this:

It's great, am I right?
It can't fail!
It's as simple as 1-2-3!
I can't believe that I was so clever and quick to come up with the plan, especially after only the five naps, four servings of leftovers,

and the three hours of back massage.

Now, time to make this all a reality! Wish me luck...!

... Well so you'll never guess what happened. It backfired!

And I don't want to talk about it anymore.

Wait, no, I want to sing about it instead!

🎵 *As you can see, That this pee,* ♪
Has been sprayed, All over me,
🎵 *Pee is not the best cologne,*
So, do you have a fur coat to loan?
♪♪

A DOG'S TAIL

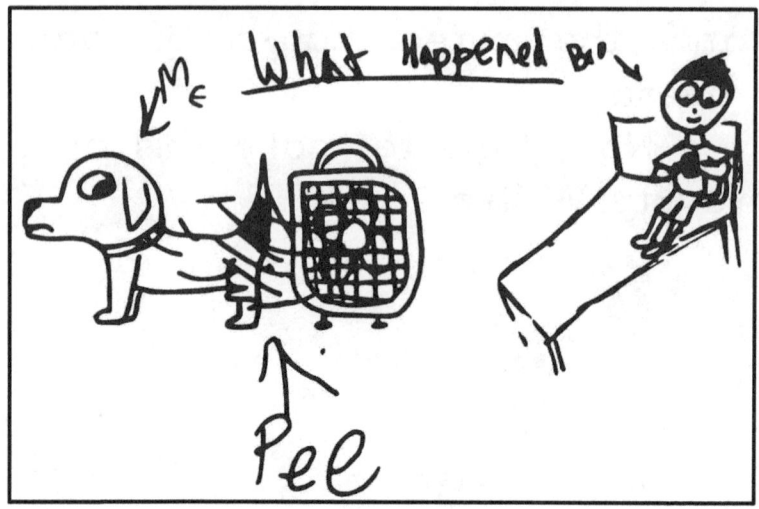

Go ahead, you can say it — I know it's true — Matchi has a lovely singing voice!

Missed Opportunity

Today I saw some meat that someone had left out on the grass. Can you imagine? They left it out on the grass! And it was some nice chicken barbeque, too! *slurp*

Ugh, I wanted it so badly.

Anyway, I sent out the signal that I trained my human pack to recognize: I rang the bell, and then I went to the garage door to wait for walkies.

A DOG'S TAIL

(Don't worry, they need the exercise, believe me.)

After many, many, many, tries they finally got the message, and my dad appeared. Then I did what I had to do:

I dragged him all the way around the house to the backyard!

We found the chicken I'd spotted, but he wouldn't let me have it. I was FURIOUS!!! That meat was calling my name! But it was what happened next that totally pushed me over the edge...

So who got the meat? A giant chicken!!! It was crazy! A giant chicken swooped down out of the sky and started eating the chicken!

Chickens eating chickens!

I didn't even know chickens could fly. Or that they got that big! Or... wait, hang on...

Um... okay, Dad is saying it's a hawk. Of course it's a hawk. I totally knew that. I was just testing you, see?

COUGH

Anyway, the point is, all the tender, juicy, delicious barbecue meat went to the dumb hawk, and it's all my dad's fault. I missed a perfectly good eating opportunity because of him.

It was a missed opportunity.

A DOG'S TAIL

Bye-Bye

Well I guess this is the end, my friend, I have told you my tale and also my tail, but, I'm still alive so maybe you'll hear about me later. Unless I get ran over by a bus or something.

Oh, I almost forgot — you're probably wondering, *how have I been writing this book?* With... my muscular and super dexterous tail, and with some ink.

A DOG'S TAIL

I *told* you us dogs were clever people.
Didn't I tell you?
I *told* you.

Afterword: Author's Note

Writing a book is harder than I thought, but, also in a way, easier than I thought. And between you and me beats homework any day. Now I'm not going to say what all the authors I've read say about them. That, "Oh, we're #1 New York Times bestseller." Yeah well I'm just a kid — that's right, a ten-year-old! Anyway, blah-blah-blah, I live in Overland Park, Kansas, with my family which includes my mom, dad, brother and me. Oh, also my dog. I mean don't blame me if I'm bad it's only my very first book, okay? How about you try juggling schoolwork and homework and everything? Okay, yeah, that's what I thought!